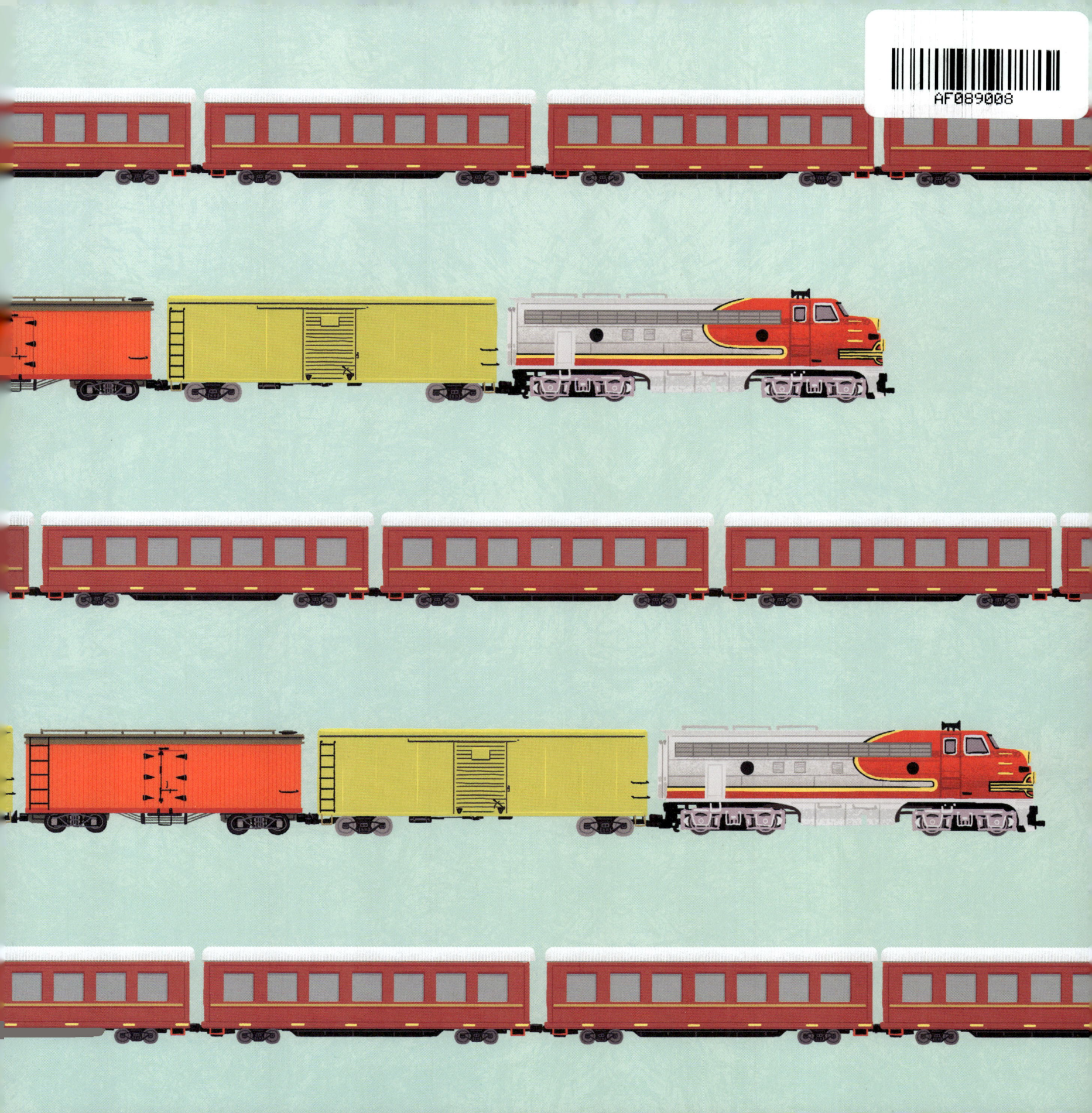

# All Aboard!

**Vicki Pipe**

Illustrated by **Joe Bucco**

WELBECK
CHILDREN'S BOOKS

# This book belongs to

..............................................

Published in 2026 by Welbeck Children's Books
An Imprint of Hachette Children's Group,
Part of the Hodder & Stoughton Limited
Carmelite House, 50 Victoria Embankment
London EC4Y 0DZ

An Hachette UK Company
www.hachette.co.uk
www.hachettechildrens.co.uk

Text © Hodder & Stoughton Limited, 2026
Illustration © Joe Bucco, 2026

Joe Bucco has asserted their moral rights to be identified as the illustrator of this Work in accordance with the Copyright Designs and Patents Act 1988.

All rights reserved. No part of this publication may be reproduced, stored in a retrieval system, or transmitted in any form or by any means, electronically, mechanical, photocopying, recording or otherwise, without the prior permission of the copyright owners and the publishers.

A CIP catalogue record for this book is available from the British Library.

HB ISBN: 978-1-7831-2936-2
E-book ISBN: 978-1-7831-2937-9

Printed in China

10 9 8 7 6 5 4 3 2 1

The authorised representative in the EEA is Hachette Ireland,
8 Castlecourt Centre, Dublin 15, D15 XTP3, Ireland
(email: info@hbgi.ie)

# Contents

Choo choo for trains! ..... 4
Freight trains ..... 6
Staying on track ..... 8
Shhhhh-steam ..... 10
Today's trains ..... 16
Travel by train! ..... 18
Bridges ..... 24
Tunnels ..... 26
Getting to the top ..... 32
Stations ..... 34
Can you spot? ..... 40

# Choo choo for trains!

Trains are one of the most exciting ways to travel in the world! They can take you to cities, through forests, under mountains, over valleys and across rivers.

to cities

across rivers

over valleys

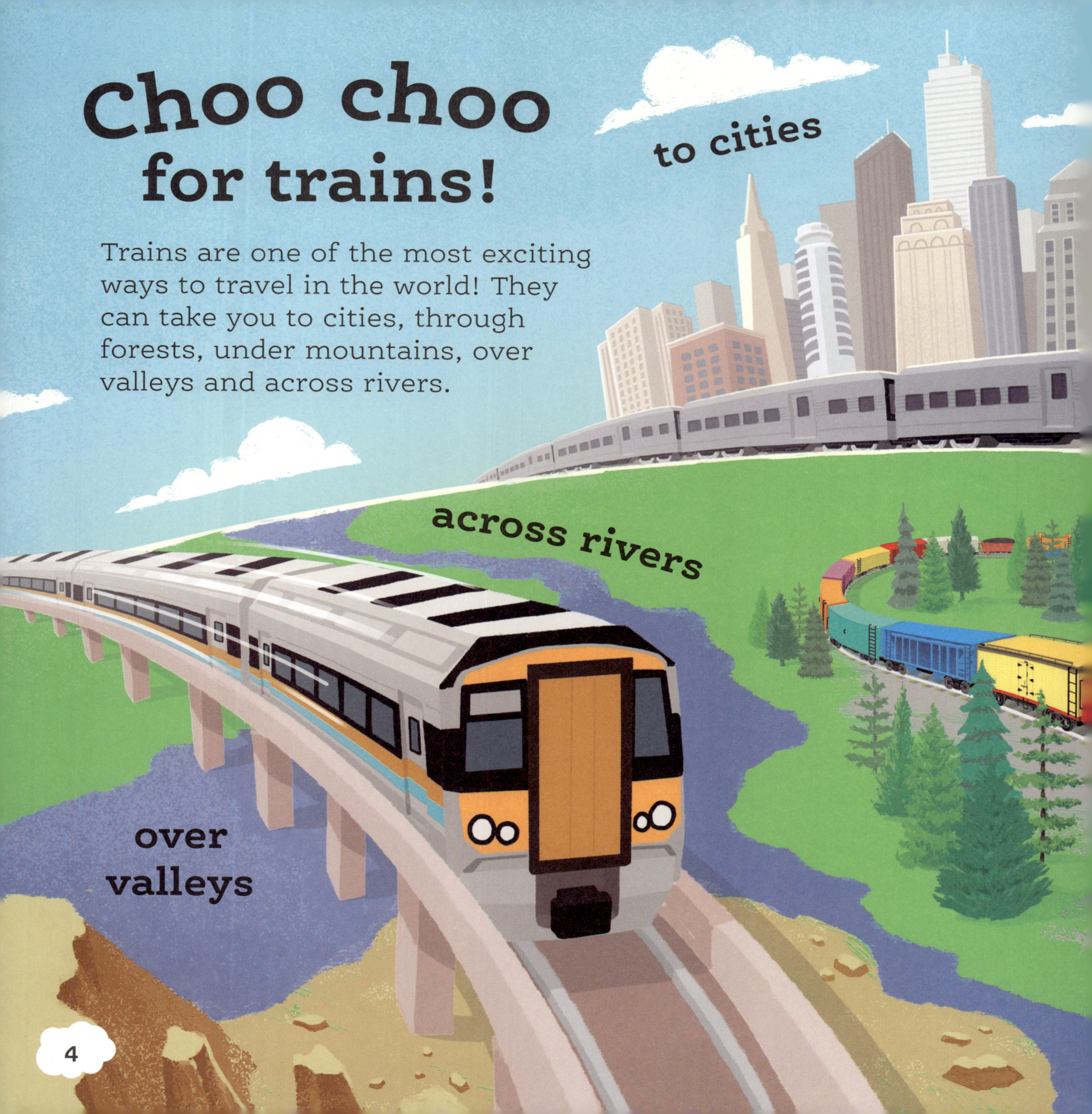

Now come with us as we take **you** on a **journey** to **discover** everything you ever **wanted** to know **about** the **wonderful** world of **trains.**

through forests

Jump aboard, and if you're ready to go, shout **'choo choo!'**

# Freight trains

Not all trains carry people, some carry things! They're called freight trains, and they can travel hundreds of miles across many countries pulling containers filled with almost anything you can imagine.

**Fruit and veg**

**Toys**

**Metals**

**Computers**

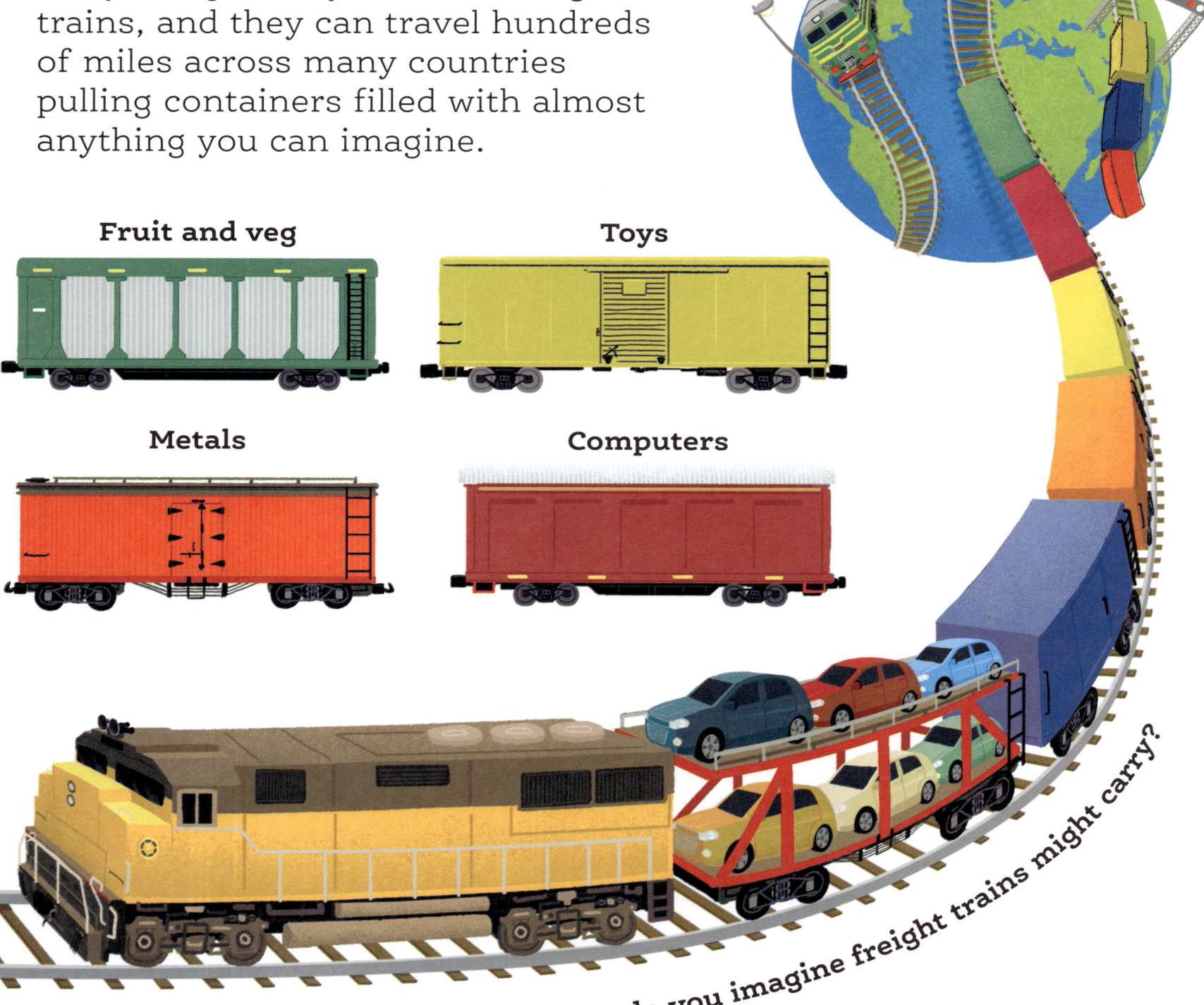

What else do you imagine freight trains might carry?

People used freight trains hundreds of years ago. They were made of wooden wagons and pulled by very strong horses – **neigh!**

The longest freight train in the world had 682 containers filled with heavy iron ore.

# Staying on track

Did you know that railways are very musical? No? Next time you're at a station listen carefully as the train gets closer, you might just hear the tracks sing!

HUMMMMMMM! HUMMMM

As the train moves the rails **hum**.

# Weather Worries

Ice and snow can cover tracks and stop trains from working safely. Special trains clear the line with snowploughs, or hot air blowers which melt the ice.

Snow plough

This rotary snow plough has propellers to push snow out of the way.

# Shhhhh-steam

Steam engines changed the railways forever, and they did it with two very special ingredients: **fire and water**.

**LET ME OUT!**

When water gets hot, it turns into steam. If you try and trap steam in a small space, it will push back as hard as it can until it finds a way to escape!

Steam engines have different names. This one's called the Mallard (like the duck). In 1938, Mallard became the fastest steam engine in the world when it reached a speed of just over 200 kilometres per hour. (This is much faster than real mallards!)

Steam is so strong it can move the largest of trains!

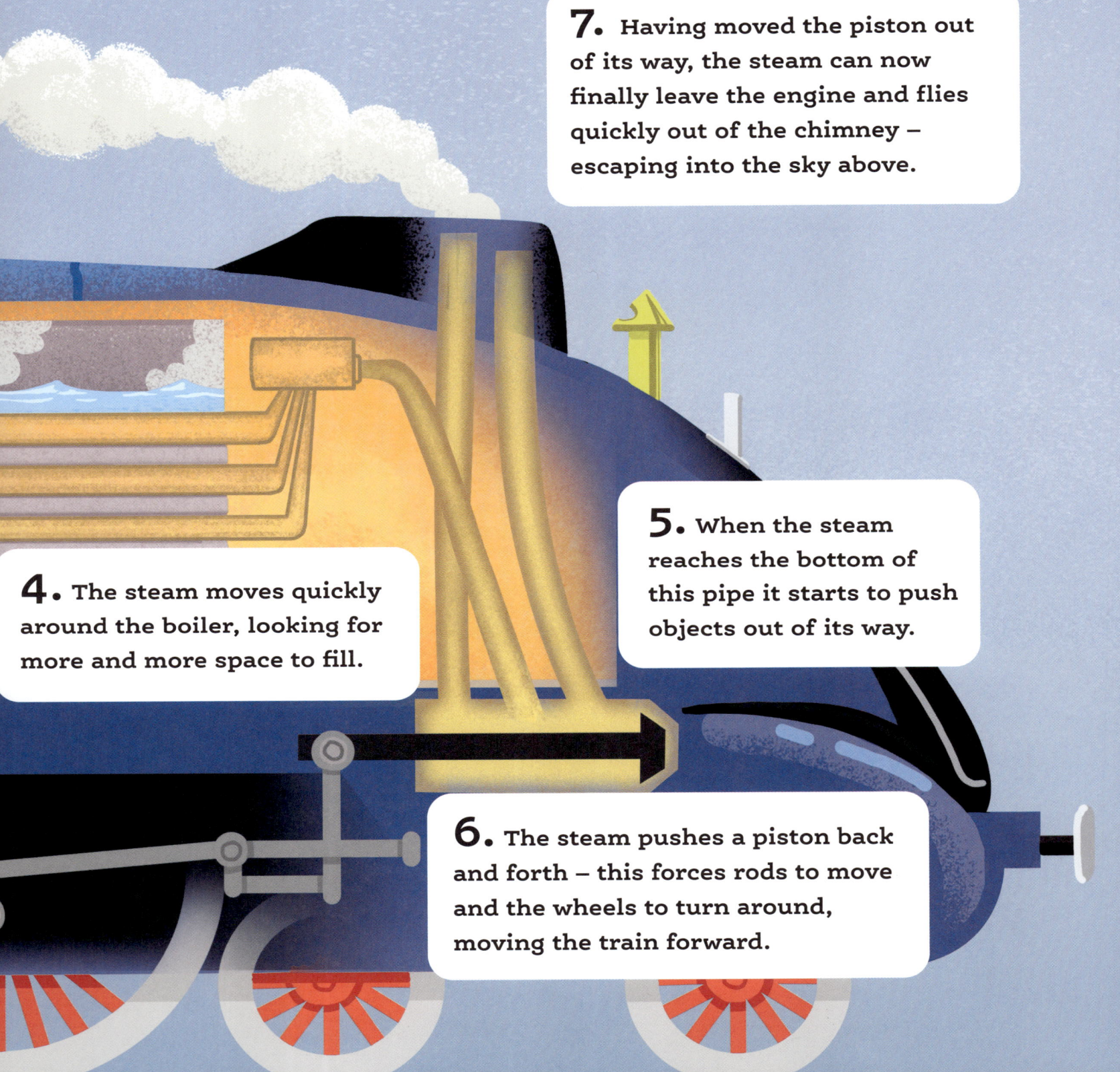

7. Having moved the piston out of its way, the steam can now finally leave the engine and flies quickly out of the chimney – escaping into the sky above.

4. The steam moves quickly around the boiler, looking for more and more space to fill.

5. When the steam reaches the bottom of this pipe it starts to push objects out of its way.

6. The steam pushes a piston back and forth – this forces rods to move and the wheels to turn around, moving the train forward.

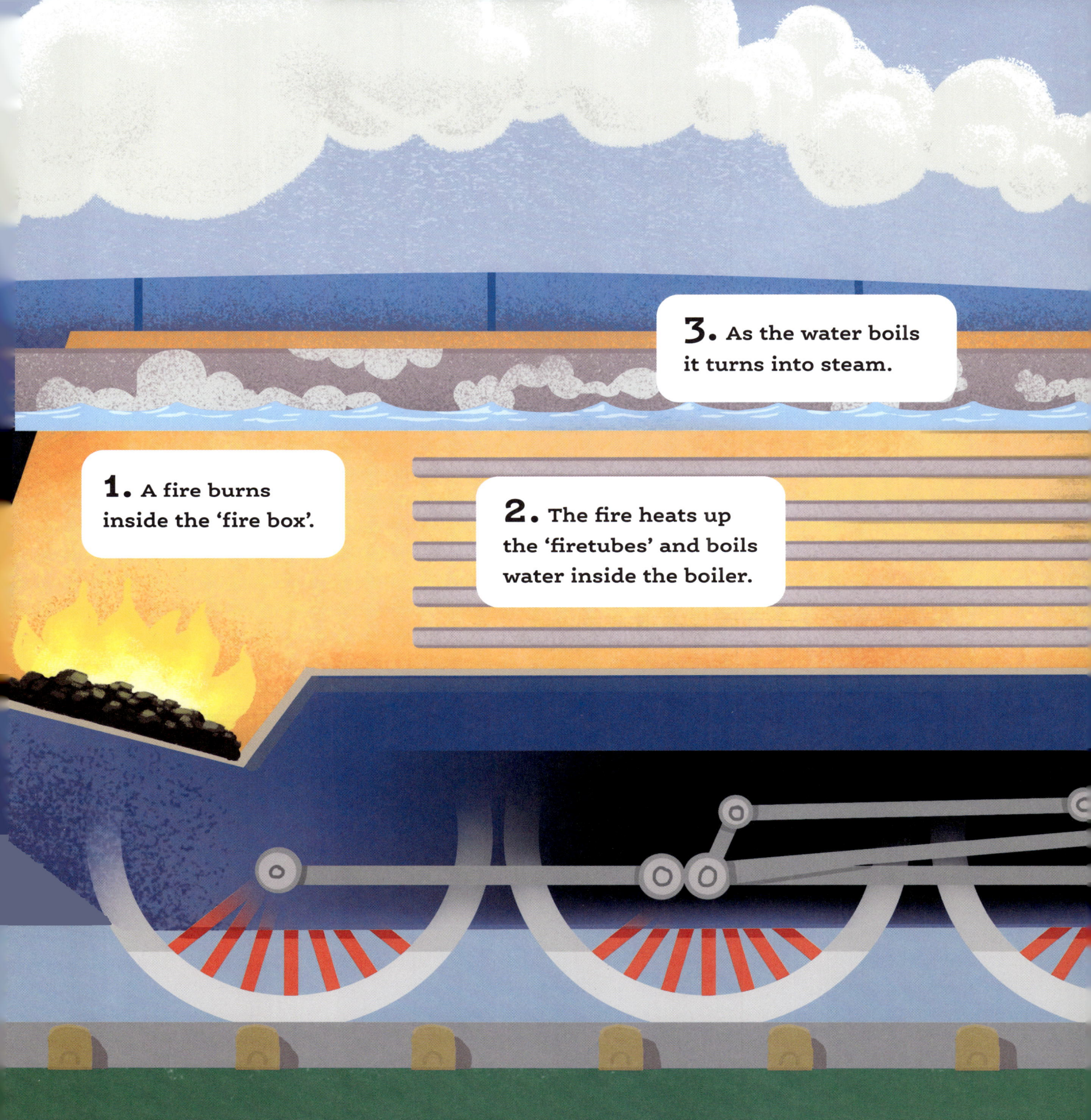

# Today's trains

Today, there are lots of different types of trains powered in lots of different ways. Some are large, some are small, some are fast, and some can even float!

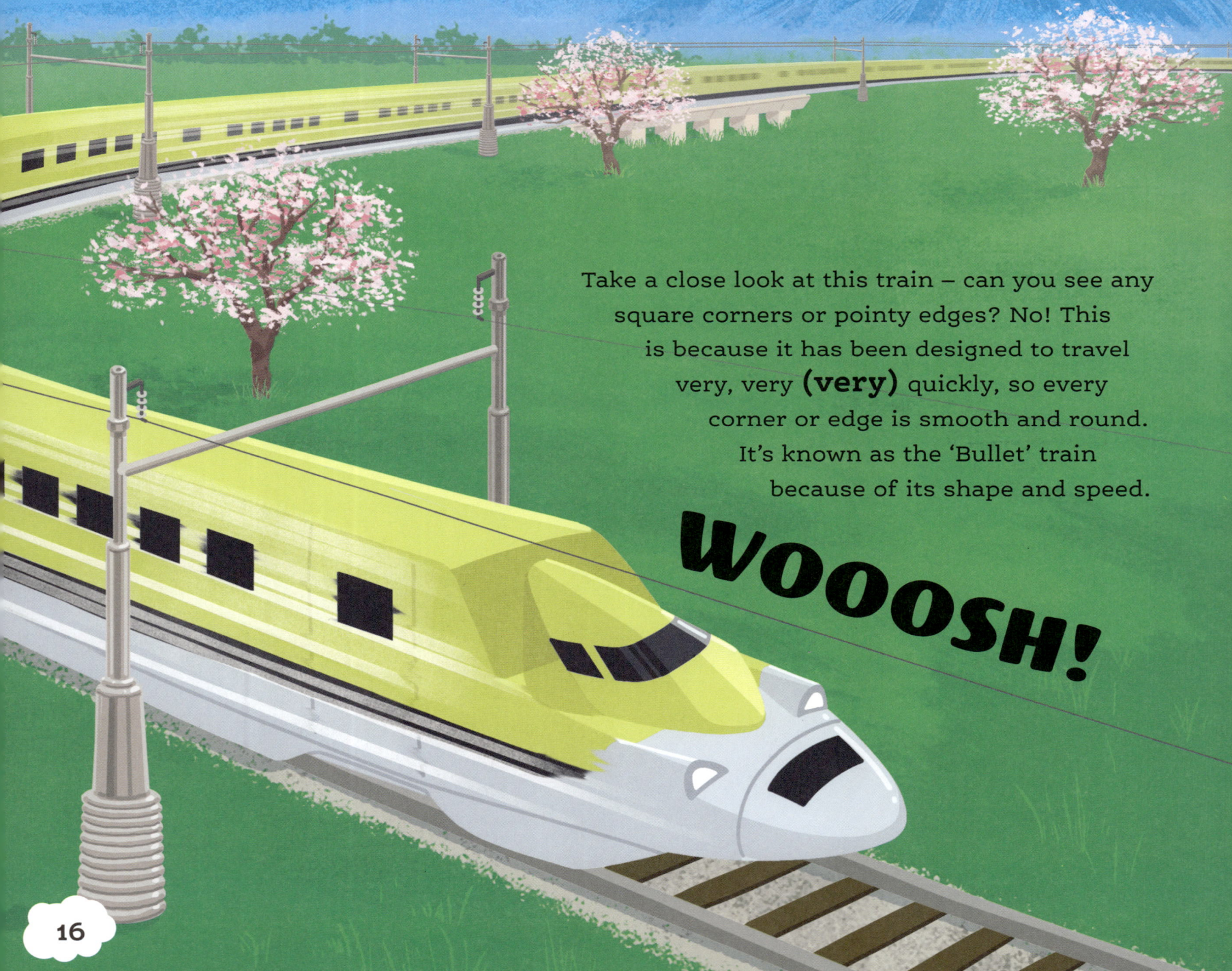

Take a close look at this train – can you see any square corners or pointy edges? No! This is because it has been designed to travel very, very **(very)** quickly, so every corner or edge is smooth and round. It's known as the 'Bullet' train because of its shape and speed.

WOOOSH!

## California Zephyr

This diesel train travels all the way across America, from one side of the country to the other. Some carriages are called 'sleeper cars', they have an upstairs and a downstairs with bedrooms where passengers can sleep, and bathrooms where they can even take a shower!

**This is the fastest train in the world**, even though it doesn't have any wheels! Instead, the train uses strong magnets that lift it right off the tracks and move it forward.

It's as if the train floats along like **magic!**

Shanghai Maglev

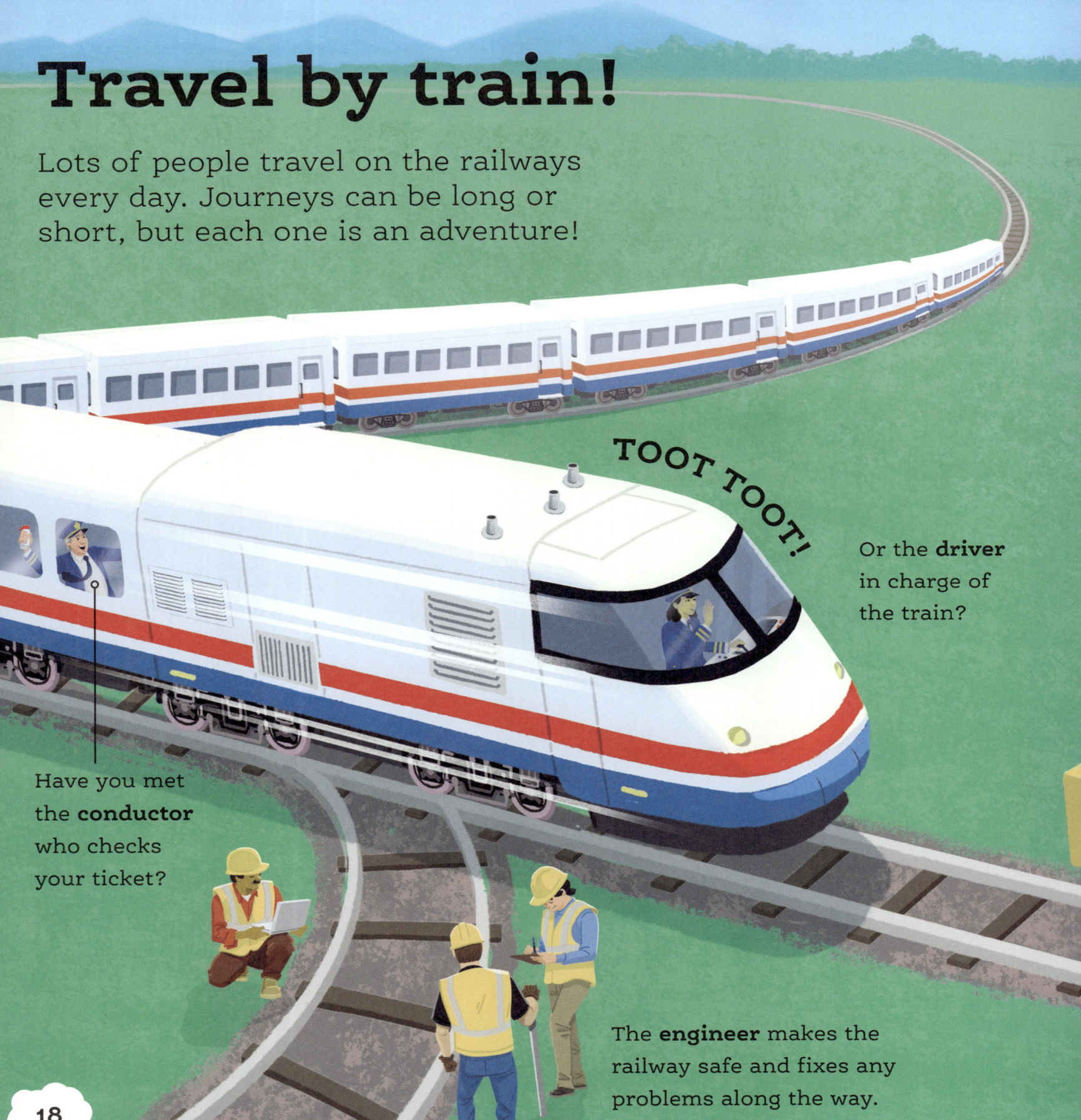

# Travel by train!

Lots of people travel on the railways every day. Journeys can be long or short, but each one is an adventure!

TOOT TOOT!

Or the **driver** in charge of the train?

Have you met the **conductor** who checks your ticket?

The **engineer** makes the railway safe and fixes any problems along the way.

18

# Bridges

What do you think happens when a railway meets a river? What about when the ground suddenly swoops down into a low valley?

Bridges are the loyal friends of the railways and will carry them through all kinds of places. Bridges come in all different shapes and sizes. Some are made from wood, some from metal, and some from super strong stone.

Viaduct

**Whirlpool Rapids Bridge**

Some bridges help trains cross into different countries. Don't forget your passport!

**The Danyang-Kunshan Grand Bridge** in China is the longest railway bridge in the whole world. It is made of a strong metal called steel and carries trains over rivers, canals, rice fields, lakes and hills for almost 165 kilometres.

# Tunnels

While some trains travel high up over rivers and valleys, other trains like to go deep down into the dark underground.

London was the first city in the world where an entire railway was built underground.

Steam trains were used and covered everything in smoke – **cough cough!**

For a long time tunnels were dug by hand, but now we use Tunnel Boring Machines.

The machine's powerful cutters at the front spin, cutting and scraping away at the earth.

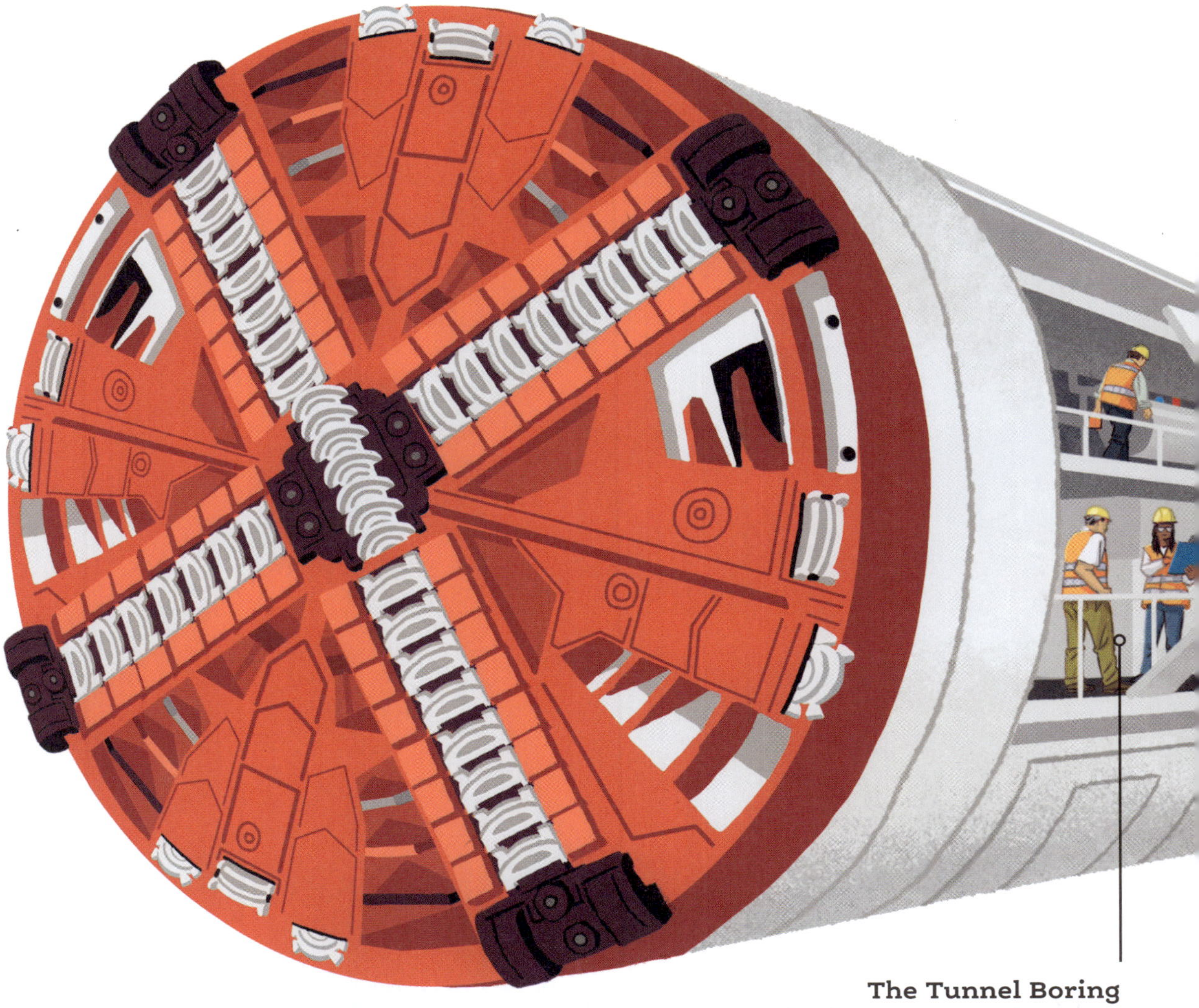

**The Tunnel Boring Machine never sleeps! Engineers keep it running all day and all night.**

The longest and deepest railway tunnel in the world is the Gotthard Base Tunnel in Switzerland. It was built under mountains and is 57 kilometres long.

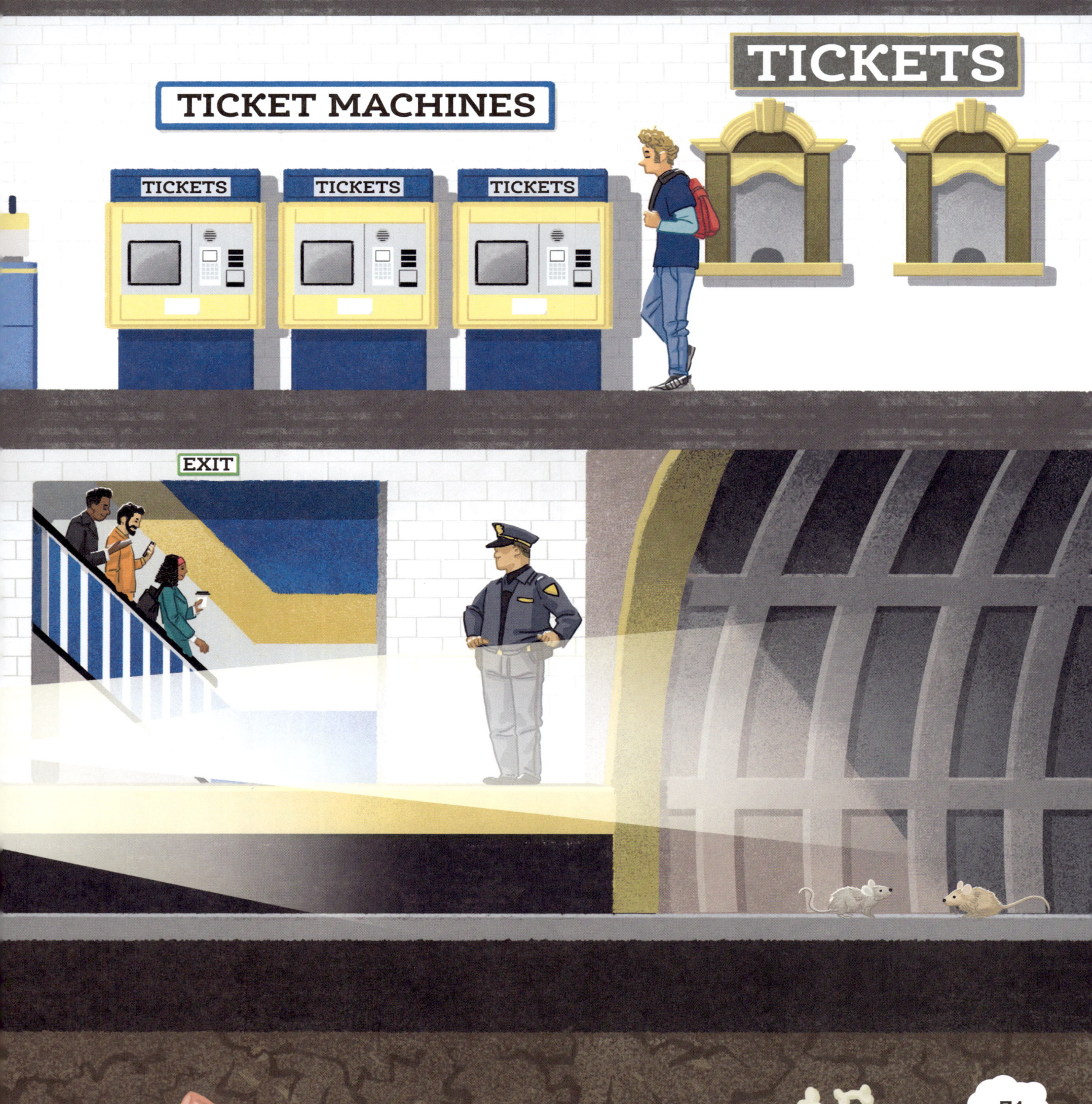

UPTOWN

# Getting to the top

As well as deep underground, railways can also be found climbing high up in the mountains and hills!

## Cable Railways

The steepest railway in the world is Katoomba Scenic Railway in Australia. The carriages on this line are pulled up and down by a very strong cable – **HEAVE!**

This train climbs hills using a special track with an extra rail. The extra rail has metal teeth that gives the train extra strength as the engine pushes the carriages up and down the hill.

This track **zig-zags** and **loops** to help trains climb through the hills! Every time the track changes direction, the train has to stop and reverse along the next bit of the line. By zig-zagging backwards and forwards the train can move up one section at a time.

# Stations

Train stations can be busy places with lots of people rushing to get to their destination. Quick – we don't want to be late and miss our train!

All the trains arriving at and departing from the station are listed on this board. Where would you like to go next?

Look out for the Information centre, where people will help you find the right platform and tell you everything you need to know about your journey.

Make sure you have your ticket ready before you get to the ticket barriers!

This machine picks up containers and moves them from one train to another.

Where will your next railway journey take you?

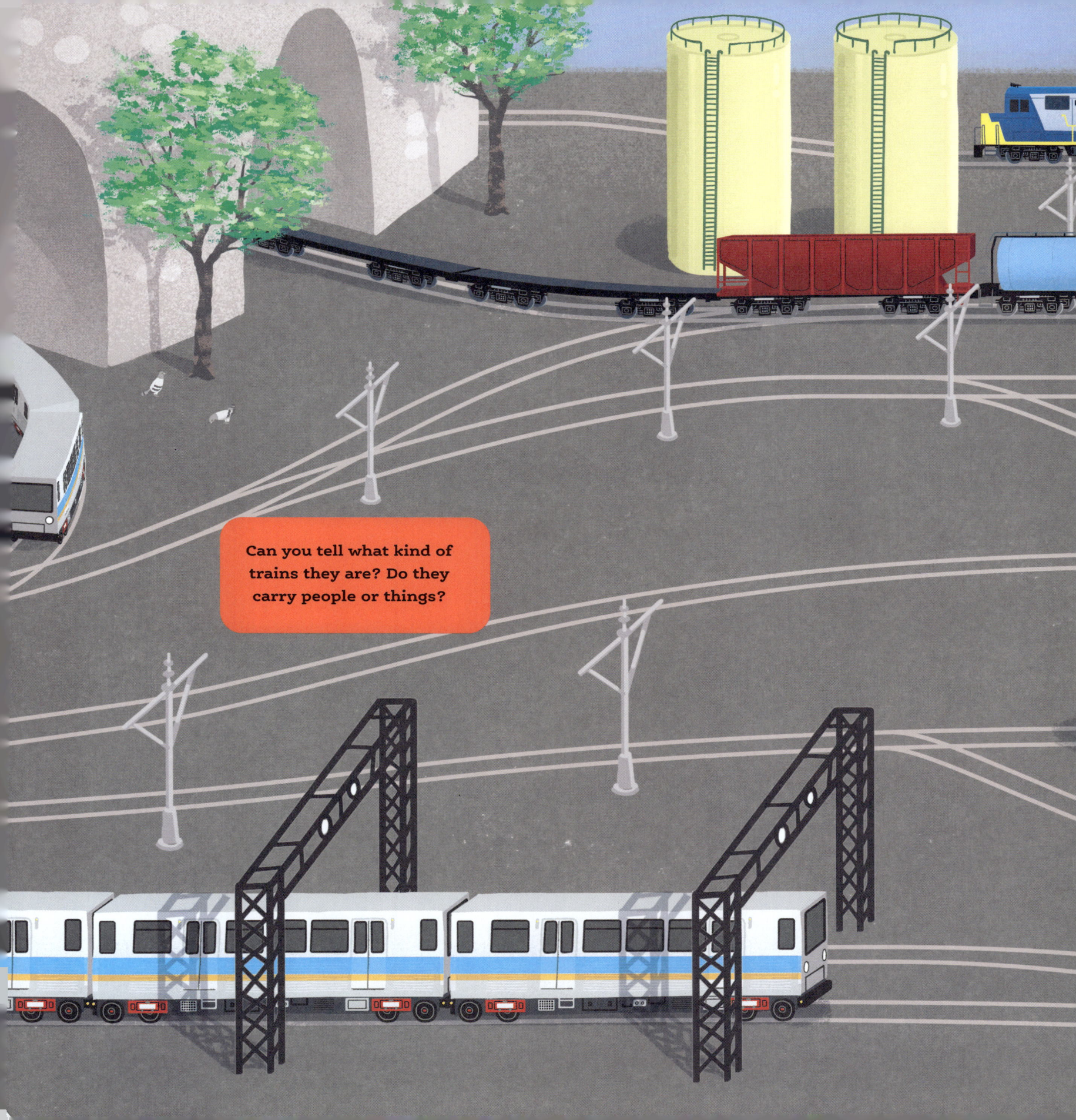

# Can you spot?

Take a look through the book and see which of these you can find!

Koala

Duck

Engineer

Cat

Suitcase

Pigeon

Fireman

Ball